WINGS WILL NOT BE BROKEN

WINGS WILL NOT BE BROKEN

by Darryl Holmes

THIRD WORLD PRESS
CHICAGO

First Edition 1990
First printing 1990
ISBN: 0-88378-137-9
Library of Congress Catalog Card #: 89-050678

Cover design by Floyd Haynes
Cover photograph by Edwin Drew

Manufactured in the United States of America

Dedication

This book is dedicated to my wonderful parents, Leah and Zurie Holmes, who struggled to keep a family together — and did!; to my three sisters, Marilyn, Zandra and Lori, and to my son, Kai Jamal Holmes, who holds my world together.

And, of course, to The Creator and the voices of the wind.

Special thanks to: John Watusi Branch (for opening the door), Amiri Baraka, Haki Madhubuti and Sonia Sanchez (for opening my eyes); Louis Reyes Rivera; Zizwe Ngafua; Ruth Garnett; Raymond Patterson; Gary Johnston; Brenda Connor-Bey; C.D. Grant; Dr. Gerald Deas; Christine Minor; Gina Minor; Edwin Drew; Lindamichelle Baron; Abiodun Oyewole; Byron Perry; Dulce Abreu... and to everyone else who believed.

Contents

Even In The Face Of Death

there are times when the moon
turns over and dies
when the sun is coy about shining
and all of the world's bullets
find a way to my soul

still I stand on African soil
In Brandfort
banished but not broken
each day a bird flies by my window
with an extra wing outstretched
with food in its mouth
and music in its soul

I understand it is a sign
when people instructed to stay away
come to me at night
with eyes big as the bread they carry
with hearts deep as a child's

never will I walk without courage
the land that consumes the dead
coughs the spirit
I inhale the rose petals
that pour from their eyes
I open my door and discover
that the earth is still the earth
and the policeman who watches
will never know how to whisper
to the insects
or pay homage to my birth
he too is banished
he believes he is doing a job
holding up a regime
that has long ago relinquished God

I feel Mandela at night
his presence enters my room
I hold his face between my palms
and pull the prison years from his eyes
our noses burst into flames
our eyes consume the fire

we rediscover the silence
and the depth of our feeling
that moves us forward
in the face of tanks and bombs
and the brutal men who fire
until blood runs in fountains
from our backs
we rediscover our commitment
to the children
who must learn to live not
as children are accustomed to living
but with the loud echo of gunfire
forever in their ears

we embrace our blackness
and blow out the candle
in the corner of the room
the policeman's pounding at the door
cannot disturb our presence
we are unashamed of the sounds we make
they are the sounds of our people
even in the face of death
the pulse of life is coming forth

Footprints (for Gwendolyn Brooks)

that you have survived
seventy years in this country
is testament
that you have turned
words into water
and water into words
that you have whispered
to guitar strings
gathered their music
washed your gardens with gold
brown black Afrikan hands

the harvest has been more than good
has nourished clothed
and collected a nation
of drummers displaced
of dancers and scientists wailing
in the diaspora

that your words have sewn
decades together
collected the history
of how we be rivers
wide back and swirling
how we be yucca and palm
pots of peppered beans
the blue light of dawn bursting forth

and no one can quiet your nostrils
or cover your hands
stop your eyes from singing
your soul from watering the land

we have grown accustomed to the brook
bold as a river
accustomed to the quietness that explodes

and your eyebrows arched
for our crossing
and your smile rippling sun
your ears swallowing every question

we thank you for the footprints
the simple and intricate patterns
the presentiments
and the power of your bones

that you have found brilliance
in the ordinary
embers in the ash
the oracle that commands this world

without your petals
we could not be nourished
without your song
we would not be whole...

Somewhere In The Dark

even as I enter the train
trying to read a newspaper
a student in South Africa
is preparing for war
even as I greet the sun
he is somewhere in the dark
drawing rifles to his chest
challenging each shadow

his heartbeat is my own
though I breathe American air
there is Bantu in my breath
though I walk with willows in these eyes
my heart is a tapestry of blood

bitter you say
but the sound of birds do not mix with guns
gold here is stained with flesh
factories lose minds in the noise of machines
and although I own no rifles
my veins are always cocked

ancient bones whisper a reunion
dry loins are raised to life
lessons pass down through
the lungs of our griots
and always the keeper of sky

even now his sweat falls from my pores
I am pacing the room
rubbing our hands together
waiting for the sound at the door

The Direction of Tide

what matters is we are friends
and if frozen and cold we come together
to call on all that is missing in our lives
let the heat draw the moon to our window
and the willingness in our hands
hold the hour still
how can we steal what is ours
how can we question the direction of tide

turn to me now
natural as the sway of palm
pull your hips to the edge of the world
where winter enters spring
and words fall silently from our pores

paint your wishes on my tongue
take me down through the years
to your birth
let me witness what it means to be a woman

I will still watch your back
as you stand spooning honey into tea
shading your breasts from the ribbons of moonlight
and the river that holds my body to the floor

Blue Smoke

baseball can bring the world together
not the bombing of children
or the blue smoke
that curls from their blood

am I wrong to cry
when others are downing beer
and whiskey
drawing the fat from the air
drowning in the streets

contradictions surround us
ironies anchored in the very words
of constitutions
why do the hungry cry for food
why must men kill for territory

perhaps it is only the score
that counts
the bottom line number
of runs arms or bodies
left on the battlefield

perhaps man is no longer civilized
or sadly mistakes civilization
for the lion's roar

beware the season of aging
unlike the sport it never ends
imbalances will be answered
with the ashes of men who fail
to remember
the earth is breathing

and those who pray by the lakes
and are humble in the presence of trees
will bring laughter to the eyes of the children
trembling in their innocence

Reflection

We became like the rest
restless in our living
I reach over the space
where you slept
memories piled high

where did they go
the galloping horses
in our veins
voices that moved our bodies
beyond the sky

your great grandmother's tears
crowd the cemetery
she floats quietly across the stone
still believing in us
in all who come together
to count the stars

we counted them once
how many winters ago
I need to remember
five years do not just blow away

I cried for your father
took my first communion
when he died
not coming to jesus
but to a man
whose face was a ferris wheel of smiles

I see him smoking cigarettes
raising chocolate cake to his mouth
the icing thick as my hand

how many years can we salvage
trying to find ourselves
I walked the way of the drum
to drown the opposition
I grew quiet at Christmas
counting the death toll in Africa
while presents were opened
at Thanksgiving I gathered
Native Americans in my bones
and blessed the table with history

you were the magnolia
blooming without direction
a summer breeze
bending the leaves

you cared without strings attached
preferring the little girl in you
to the woman
and I welcomed this
but could not walk away
from what a black man feels
when his eyes are fully open

if I stayed the same
we would still be singing
somewhere caribbean
the wine coolers in our hands

I would not be counting
the steps of our son from a distance
or drowning in the path he walks

No, all women are not the same Sabrina
every man is not an airplane
waiting to take off

Haiku

the peeled fruit of us
lies on an empty table
touching shamelessly

Contents

When The Water Rushes

come lay your feet upon the earth
I am every bit the man you married
maybe more

though I have learned
to keep company with the sun
to sing strange blues
near the bathroom window
to travel while standing still
stalking the heartbeat
that has been with me since birth

I am every bit the journey
you embarked on
every bit the tide
that rolls gently to the shore

the sand still holds our footprints
each season I return
to run my hands along the lines
to listen to the wind change direction
the rocks break their silence

each season I leave looking back
before going forward
focusing the earth's evolution
the way a lake becomes a mirror
in spring
or a caterpillar becomes a butterfly

I have not forgotten
how to measure your universe
to lay a bed of roses beneath your head
to call on the heat
of our very first winter
when we dared to skate undressed
along the ice

even now I am conscious of these things
the way a drowning man is conscious
of dying
the way a cat ponders a hole
before springing for its prey
the way a baby watches shadows
rise and fall in a room

If there is to be a rekindling
a second season of surrender
where love is a steady flow
we must not stand in the way
of water when it rushes
welcome the movement
dive into the center
where secrets are born

Union Song

it is more than the thought
of physical fire
though our union could cause
the darkness to quake

it is a question of length
and time
of turning on the crest
of a constant wave
wetting sand and stone

of stretching our limbs to lock
in the midst of morning mud
rising to spill the rain across our eyes

One Chord (for Malcolm)

holidays hold no weight
less we wear them like
our loins
maybe it is better Malcolm
America is afraid
of unfolding your bones

bullets never die
but rise out of flesh
to flood the rivers
where your nostrils
hardened to steel hang
smoking

eighteen years
have not cooled the irons
or caused our eyes to stutter
like bat wings

we come wearing our music
with banners in our eyes
and blood
for breaking along the current
where we come
to collectively raise the coffin

your name chanted
like new words
from a child's lips
overlaps the sun
we praise your brilliance
press the waters against our voice

one chord
cutting
with oriental precision
a stronger path

this is a sacred celebration
of fragmented hairs
brought together by your hands
we are holy here Malcolm
cornrowed along the river

missing pages of testament

For The Same Reasons

the stones I bear
cannot brace me for the weight
of your convictions
it is only your voice
wailing in the darkness
a million years of womanhood coming down

I am dying inside
for the same reasons that women die
love is walking backwards in the dark
men do not always breathe without heart
or blood

bleed with me this hour
while pale silhouettes
are walking through my bones
the last candle burns a sweet perfume

find me in the morning
moving my wings against the sun
searching for rainbows
outside the reach of familiar arms

invite me to stay
or throw your foolish stones until I fly

Gooseberry Eyes

it has been a long time Lillian
since we left the waters
of your country
to come back home
the sea is forever turning grey

I can find your footprints
along the beach
the brown eyes that fell
like crushed plums
upon the sand
and the lines
that open and close
on your forehead

so many years of peddling
the protracted struggle
to stay alive
as middle woman
as wife
walking between
the powdered bones of peasants
who hold their songs beneath the earth
you are one with their voices
though your vowels contract
in the presence of strangers

"one for fifteen
two for twenty-five"

the sun dresses
cotton cloth blushing
with the colors of berry and grape
of mango and coconut
of banana and yam

and in the yard
your daughter draws a dress
that is eleven years old
and the man you move
closer to at night
has not forgotten how
to lift your wings
or wash you down in holy water

it is the land that is missing
the fuller bowl of rice*
that Rivera speaks about
the blood that returns to the people
who have planted generations
in the soil

oh Bajan woman
you are not alone in your hunger
for truth to return
I too have gooseberry eyes
and bowels that long to be emptied

I too relinquish the sweat
and cannot smell the flower
unless the moon is full
or the factory has been washed
from my breath

we have been here before
though the balance seems
more uneven now
maybe it is the cataracts
coming before their time
or the millions of backs
that are turned to the sea...

* Louis Reyes Rivera, from a poem entitled "Constant"

A Time For Guns
(in memory of Martin Luther King, Jr.)

would I have marched with you Martin
moved to the color and cadence of your voice
rolled with your vowels into consonants
coming on like waves

would I have blown fire from these fists
faced the twisted mouths of murderers
turned the other cheek
as they chastised me with hose

nineteen years after your death
after they blew you from a balcony
and the butterflies fell from your bones
nineteen years after the earth stood still
and a movement staggered across America
the stones are still coming

the cries of Birmingham children
are broken by Atlanta
the blue sky is scarred with blood
and the bones of Eleanor Bumpers
are breathing for justice here Martin

would I have marched
knowing the faces you met
still move in Forsyth County
where klansmen demonstrate
against your holiday
knowing that Arizona is rescinding
her conscience
and Reagan is riding cavalry
into the hills of Nicaragua

I believe in mountaintops
in the blue water of our birth
in the brown bodies that built this country Martin
but we walk alone in our quest for peace

those in power do not surrender to spirit
do not meditate on trees or the fruit they bear
they believe in alternatives Martin
maybe it is time for guns...

Somewhere Stephen Biko

on this night beating with rain
this cold night absent of moon
beating with rain
i remember Stephen Biko
standing on the pulse of apartheid
with only his voice in search of victory
there are no violins
no grand pianos
only a cappella pounding from a rock
poems splitting stones
Samora's tears turning yellow on the page

death was no mystery
let the lesions in his brain
speak to this
let his eyes crowded with blows
his teeth trapped in silence
settle the questions
because he believed in consciousness
carrying our own voice to battle
trusting in the bones that sing to us
sun up and sun down if we listen

this man who could see sideways
reach farther than the years
that numbered his life
wash a white man down in his own religion
and leave him to falter or die

not even a thousand tanks
can crush his promise
not even a million soldiers
who sing through Botha's eyes

and the dawn dusts off his voice
and the dusk drinks
from the river where we stand
with palms open like guns
and we gather his spirit
and polish his laughter to balance the blood
and the rain
on this night beating with rain

and somewhere Coltrane is blowing
After The Rain
and we call on the Afro Blue
in us
on the Biko in us
the bridges and ancient pyramids
in us
after the rain
on this night speaking roughly in my ear
i empty this song

and there are loins
in the throats of the children
drumbeats in their loins
elephants
leaping boldly from their eyes

not one is turning back
or washing her bones in the river
or turning his eyes in the blood
that circles his hands

and somewhere Bob Marley is singing
a redemption song
and somewhere Stephen Biko
is freeing the land.

Birth Song

I have watched your waist
like the hands of a clock
slowly swell between the bliss
no one says it is a boy
only our blood entwined
the softer berry of the tribe
they have come to know!

what matters is that you are ripe
it could rain on the second day
or the seventh
but it will rain

the roads we walked will reappear
the trees will shake like tamborines
the earth will dance
until the Gods are weary of praise

part of you part of me
a morning without confusion
a night where we bathe
in the moon between your breasts

Another Color

She said the color of my eyes
ain't purple
I can still hear him cry at night
can still hear him cry

nobody ever called him mister
or lifted the hammer
long enough for him to breathe
still on the boat that brought us here
rocking bones through the stench
of a journey
joining eyes to the absence of moon
and the memory of sun

all his songs in my ear
all his anger turned to love
in this body of bushes and trees
my bones are trembling

don't speak to me of blood
unless outside the circle
I share with this man
don't speak to me of pain
when Charlie sold his horn
Muddy lost his blues
Billy dropped her bones
on the wings of a butterfly
it's all they could do

every color can't be purple
every dance does not lead
to the drawing of blood
takes guts
to gravitate towards wings
takes a man and woman

a singular motion through mud
and rain
a resurrection of spirit
a belief in love again

don't speak to me of colors
that fail to bring us closer
I come to resurrect kings
not cut them down

Butterflies

I am unsettled now
an ocean
after the boats have gone
a sky without recurring moons
only memories

your head lifted toward the sun
Ankh of ivory
eyes echoing Egypt
lips soft as the land
giving way to laughter

only a long hard stare in the wind
will awaken me
only the beating of hearts
or the hurricane
that crosses our cities

you are sacred
morning prayer beneath my pillow
painting of horizons
I've longed to hold

help me with these feelings
full like the wings of a dove
or the arms of a dancer
steady these pores
pulsing with rain
and the reckless dance of heart

hold me close to the fire
the butterflies are beating
only your brown wings
can rescue me now

Between Two Mountains

upon my leaving
I look to the wind for your face
and find it floating
across a fading sunset
to reinflame the sky

these Pennsylvania mountains
move me closer to myself
I contemplate the return to cities
the scent of sweet oils
rising from your pores

here I have eaten from the fruit of myself
and from the many who have gathered
to grow whole in the sight of God

I am hearing your voice
venetian blinds beating in the bedroom
Kai's cries
rising over young teeth
that torment his gums

you come at a time
when the rain reopens her eyes
to release her sons
and daughters to the earth
to unfold the leaves of flowers
bent in prayer

I look to green hills
that have healed us
knowing that we will come back
breathing the Afrocentric song
with fuller lungs
knowing that I will kiss

the welcome from your lips
and lay three days of living in your hands
to hold me still

your love rocks the ground on which I walk
it has always done so
only now I have learned to hear the trembling

take me in your arms when I return
brace me for the full breath of this country
that cleans its teeth with our bones
balance me like the mountains of Pennsylvania
suddenly, I am anxious to come home

there is always room
for old trumpet players in heaven
let them hear your full-bellied sound
not the silence that washes
against my memory
or the mist that moved you from the crowd

poems sometimes cry like trumpets
crease the wind
with a metaphor of tears
turn to paraphrase a marching band
blowing poignant blues
for the passing of a brother

I breathe a baritone spirit
splicing the weight of our eyes
open hands we held together in the sun
seasons of sharing books bread
and the braided dreams of men
drawn together by God

there are memories to gather
flowers to fill a room
a faint rumbling under earth
where ancient hands help your spirit
through the soil

I see you walking on the face of a river
blowing October leaves against the moon
lamenting the return of Miles
electric blues

hear you wailing from red horizons
raising acoustic riffs to walk the sun
there are voices beyond the mountains
there are moments still to come

Raise My Eyes

down here where men
draw breath from stone
I stand in a pool of silence
slicing my veins with victories
and defeats

who will hear me now
climbing down the chimneys
with cold dust in these lungs
large sacks filled with the bones
of an African child

what is more holy than hands
stretched across the Atlantic
or a loud song
from the muddy waters of our weeping

raise my eyes above the ribbons
I am reaching deeper than decoration
into the dark folds of famine and drought
into a future that staggers
like a blind man in mourning
missiles hanging from his mouth

I embrace the beauty
that brought us through the years
to conquer cane and cotton
to marry by jumping brooms
brush the night with naked bodies
and bashful moons

raise my eyes above the ribbons
where Robben Island aches
with the weight of Mandela's will
and resistance reaches into

the deepest part of the blood
where students stand
in the memory of Stephen Biko
and women breathe songs over burning coals

hear them chanting incantations
stretching loins over deserts
dividing their time
between lovemaking and war

whispers in the bush
a commitment to cornrows and killing
to the cleansing of African earth
and the restoration of the river
and its people

raise my hands to reach
the elephant tusks
in hours of weakness
when my souls are spitting fire
and the fertile soil of a legacy
is being challenged by facade

raise my eyes to rest
in the belly of the sky
with blue mountains
a slow burning sun
red orange rhythms ancient
as time

J.J.

J.J. I think of you now
natural mystic
nostrils the diameter of coins
your speech carries back to the road
the cars turning up dust

pulling on spliff for inspiration
you spoke to the rocks
and the ocean that anoints them
I away from home
bound by your blackness
teeth white as moon
eyes of muddy water washed in flame

I hold the flint stone in my hand
and know we are connected
Montego Bay has its beggars
America, its men without homes
the same hands stir both countries

in the land of the sun
children sell their faces
in the land of the gun
bodies are sold

so many television dreads
so many crooked songs
and soldiers dead at birth

still you are clear
to claim thirteen children
from five different drums
dance with your ear to the ground
your mouth to the mineral spring
sun stalker

burning spear
barracuda black man
breathing strong syllables

I hold your song in heart
hunger for the cadence of speech
mangoes we burst in the rain
the ride into hills holy with trees

you touch the ocean in different places
hustle the unconscious
travelers like me
we will find you J.J.
wherever the water trembles
wherever the earth moves
and the sane are mad enough to scream

For Mbembe

I hear you louder
than I ever have before Mbembe
but must the loudest cry
always be the last

so often you spoke of playing "side-two"
life was no exception
you have landed
we are left to contemplate the reasons
protect the poems that pull thin the loins
bleeding is easy
for a brother who merits blood

but how do I sing Mbembe
bring your words back to the people
plant your wisdom in stone
for the many who will travel future roads
in search of truth

tell me where you laid your pipe to rest
how you swallowed the sound of your voice
to plunge so passionately to the ground

tell me how can I reach you
what tree or stream must I follow
what bird that bends its wings to brush the sky

give me a sign Mbembe
we can breathe a duet across the dawn
and bathe in the holy hour of awakening

The Holiest of Dances

love is the landscape of a woman
stretching across continents
to kiss the fever from my bones
a brown wind
wrapping curtains of clean air
around the midriff of morning
where peace is still
and poems celebrate the blueness of sky

love is the last time I touched her
the eyes she opened up like rain
the river that washed our voices
to the shore
the sweet gentle meaning of her name

lips like pillows
pushing down against the darkness
the blue perfume of her body
being the only light

we linger here
where language is primordial
pulling from the essence of ourselves
earthly branches
breathing soft against the night
merging to cornrow a rhythm
out of rain and sun
the surface of our mouths trembling

we come here to confirm our living
to lay footprints
on the petals of an hour
forever opening to rain
it is the holiest of dances
to match love's every move
until the mountains cease to sway

Disembark (for Gwendolyn Brooks)

1

we descended from the clouds
into clear water blue
where boats bear the birth
of infant waves
and the wind lies dormant
in the sun
south sea island
a room with ocean view.
hear the voices of the sea
luring me to coral reefs
past coconut palms
and powdered sand
where native sons salute
from wooden docks.
I wear these waters like a shawl
from shallow to deep
the shore grows distant
sun's arms extend to touch
tiny fish fly through open fingers
I fill my trunks with shells.
alone with sky and sun
this water washing clean
like the wisdom of God
no one paints like God.

2

behind the beauty
who hears the call of the Arawak
climbing out of conch shells
to caress the cays
winding through wealth and want
(near Prince George Wharf)
where women weave their sisal fiber
and palmetto plait

into purses and shoes
Bahamian women
who bargain until you buy
bathe in the shadow of slanted roofs
they watch
and sometimes admire tourists
flaunting ancient airs
and tans that will peel
when the planes pull down.
they know of husbands
selling fish and fruit
driving jitneys into Bay street
their boys and girls
guarding coins that contribute
to evening meals
it can be dark inside the sun.

3

restless drumbeats stroke the air
the Arawak are singing
drawing darkness from the sun
dancing their ritual.
red dust runs from bones
bilingual waters return to the sea
Afrikan footsteps
swallow the odor of guns
a gathering in blue
a drum a bow an arrow a shield
shadows dancing into flesh
firm thighs facing questions
bodies on the verge of disembark...

let their voices carry the song
weave a new circumference out of memory
make a promise to the earth

let no other hands enslave the soil.

83 Winters (for my grandmother)

if there is beauty to be found
it is in the quiet passing
of her birth
from flesh to spirit
her bones bend softly in the wind

83 winters have witnessed her crossing
a cream-colored journey
along the cracked and broken sides
of a city
where her baptist singing voice
raised the roofs off of churches
and charmed eleven children from her womb

we come to bear witness
to walk the final corridor
creased with the lines of her living
each with our memories
her gray hair sprouting seeds
her small black eyes embedded
in moonlight
her fine red lips

we come because crying is necessary
because death is not only a divider
but a multiplier of moans

we move shoulder to shoulder
balancing boats upon our hips
holding her favorite hymns between our bones
breathing hard to hold back the noise

never again will she walk before our eyes
unless we believe in God's spirit
never again will she whisper

of her 83 winters
or the autumns that embraced her
with brown and yellow leaves

never will she dance in brown shoes
shout with imaginary friends
or share her painted wings
unless we turn in the direction of the sun
and witness the possibilities

then the boats will slide down
from our hips
and we will hear the sound of motors
and smell the scent of pot roast
and buttered yams

we will hear her oatmeal
puffing in aluminum pots
and ride her gentle voice
beyond the cold and misty valleys
where magenta and lilac lace the sky

until we settle like the dew over morning
softening the ground for her return
measuring our lives against the goodness
that is falling
as the sun's golden arms impact the dawn

Generations

world don't like
no angry colored man
son
shoot em in the groin
where grassroots grow
amidst future seeds

say we s'pose to like
shining shoes
wit' wide smiles
spread across our face
large like piano keys

ain't never stop cuttin' cane
in they eyes
still watermelon boys
and wenches
wide lip peoples proud
of nothin' but the way we dance

these marks on my back
thick
like railroad tracks
crossing every which way

feel em son
run your growin' hands
'cross the welts
know my naked screams
when they were raw
hear my eyes
crumble like coal dust
and your daddy
loadin' up his gun

we been blacksmiths
cooks
builders and farmers
preachers of the word of God

we been soldiers
railroad runners
healers with our herbs
backbone of a race breakin' down
defenders of the family

we been men son

we been men

Praise Poem (for Dr. Deas)

I have watched you
drag the irons from the river
rocking back and forth
forth and back
to steady yourself for the fire

I have seen you with cities on your back
breathing new rain
to rinse the dust of quiet decades
from our eyes

I have heard you singing
on the edge of sleep
sliding between the barricades of a country
increasingly bent on war
and I have wondered what a man it takes
to move mountains upon his lungs
and laugh to keep the solemn chords
from crashing down

and although I am not a singer
I want to sing for you
an unrehearsed solo
sliding across the centuries of pain
where proud spirits splice the wind
with our echoes
and ancient chants fall like sacred rain

I want to paint for you an evening
red with sun
a morning moving life
across the fertile bones of bridges
a dusk drinking
from the deep blue well of your birth

Mokoena (for Elizabeth Mokoena)

I bleed from every pore that opens
to pronounce your name Mokoena
never to know your nineteenth birthday
or shake your belly in the wind
when the white man falls

the air is still
at the bus stop in Bethlehem (South Africa)
where you balanced your breath
between questions
and called to your mother in silent code

I die each time I think of your death
each time I hear the truck's wheels turn
the white boys move behind their whiskey
the blood of Botha and Vorster in their veins

I carry the shame of cousins
who stood constricted by history
who wanted desperately to be men
they still walk with ice in their blood
wake to eyes wildly blinking
wear the tread marks in the road

I reach down
anchor myself in Afrika
wail from the lungs of women
whose bodies shake with stones
whose bones hold the noise of your journey
the jagged pounding of apartheid

one after another
Wessels
Mynhardt
Swanepol

Viljoen
one after another
pressing perverted rifles between your legs
exploding with the absence of culture
or commitment to God

and you struggled to gather your blouse
and the screams that roared
from the bottom of the universe
and the bottle crashing against your head

and you cried for the little girl in you
for the ribbons and bows
for the geles and bubbas
for the time behind the womb
when the world blew songs along the umbilicus
and no one could touch you

still they turned around
afraid of how your mouth would open
how your loins would rattle
along the roadside
and your eyes would bury the sun

your body became a fountain
opened by the fishing knife
and the filthy hands of Wessels
and the filthy eyes of his ancestors
and the numbered days of a regime
that will wear the hoof marks
of warrior's horses

hear them coming Mokoena
to overturn the mud
and lift the tread marks from your torso
it must come to this
there is no other way that we
or the white man will understand

Wings Will Not Be Broken

I will not live
to see the last tooth
topple into basin
these black hands sucked dry
like raisins to reach
there are so many bullets in the air

bullets born of bastard minds
men who stroke the heads
of burning rockets
blast off into space
from spawning rooms
where windows have no voice
and computers cough their signals of success

it is hard to keep sane hard
but only the stillborn stone
the wings of birds
and tamper with the seasons
say thou shall not kill
while dropping cluster bombs
to clarify aggression

who are we kidding
better ourselves than the children
who should not have to weep
when we already know
who should not have to weep
when we already know the danger

of not finding ourselves
when we need to look
so many still waiting for the hurricane
of a Harlem Renaissance
or the riots of Watts

so many still looking for Malcolm
under the moon
when his words should be the rain
that waters our days
and dances up a bush fire in broken hearts

so many have fought and died
and fought and died
and died and fought

the teeth of european dogs digging through bone
like buzz-saws through bark

and fought and died

tear gas turning eyes to ghosts
and hearts into hostages
of hueless pitch and tone

and died and fought

the bullet
deity of the dragon
who continues to stalk the land
laughing through layers of ice
the dragon who gives birth to nothing
but death and destruction
lying about the labor pains and pyramids
has stolen a children and bludgeoned a history
Unholy are the raids

but this is not a poem of pure pain
and purple hearts bleeding blue light

have fought and died

have fought and fought
are fighting and killing

resilience roots us
in the retina of the storm
each day that we live
the dragon grows weary

unlike the Indians
we are still around in numbers
that haunt his heated nostrils
and drive him to drawing boards
of darker destruction

even the pyramids haunt him
and he pukes in lonely rooms
where laughter is a million miles away

he is afraid of Saxophones and Trumpets
of Cowbells and Kalimbas
he is afraid of Drums
especially the Drums

he sleeps on iron pillows
and peeks with putrid eyes
through each new dawn, wondering

if the roaring Nile has reached his doorstep

ALSO AVAILABLE FROM THIRD WORLD PRESS

Nonfiction

The Destruction Of Black Civilization: Great Issues Of A Race From 4500 B.C. To 2000 A.D.
by Dr. Chancellor Williams $16.95

The Cultural Unity Of Black Africa
by Cheikh Anta Diop $14.95

Home Is A Dirty Street
by Useni Eugene Perkins $9.95

Black Men: Obsolete, Single, Dangerous?
by Haki R. Madhubuti
paper $14.95
cloth $29.95

From Plan To Planet Life Studies: The Need For Afrikan Minds And Institutions
by Haki R. Madhubuti $7.95

Enemies: The Clash Of Races
by Haki R. Madhubuti $12.95

Kwanzaa: A Progressive And Uplifting African-American Holiday
by Institute of Positive Education
Intro. by Haki R. Madhubuti $2.50

Harvesting New Generations: The Positive Development Of Black Youth
by Useni Eugene Perkins $12.95

Explosion Of Chicago Black Street Gangs
by Useni Eugene Perkins $6.95

The Psychopathic Racial Personality And Other Essays
by Dr. Bobby E. Wright $5.95

Black Women, Feminism And Black Liberation: Which Way?
by Vivian V. Gordon $5.95

Black Rituals
by Sterling Plumpp $8.95

The Redemption Of Africa And Black Religion
by St. Clair Drake $6.95

How I Wrote Jubilee
by Margaret Walker $1.50

A Lonely Place Against The Sky
by Dorothy Palmer Smith $7.95

Fiction

Mostly Womenfolk And A Man Or Two: A Collection
by Mignon Holland Anderson $5.95

Sortilege (Black Mystery)
by Abdias do Nascimento $2.95

Poetry and Drama

To Disembark
by Gwendolyn Brooks $6.95

I've Been A Woman
by Sonia Sanchez $7.95

My One Good Nerve
by Ruby Dee $8.95

Geechies
by Gregory Millard $5.95

Earthquakes And Sunrise Missions
by Haki R. Madhubuti $8.95

Killing Memory: Seeking Ancestors
by Haki R. Madhubuti $8.00

Say That The River Turns:
The Impact Of Gwendolyn Brooks
(Anthology)
Ed.by Haki R. Madhubuti $8.95

Octavia And Other Poems
by Naomi Long Madgett $8.00

A Move Further South
by Ruth Garnett $7.95

Manish
by Alfred Woods $8.00

New Plays for the Black Theatre
(Anthology)
edited by Woodie King, Jr. $14.95

Children's Books

The Day They Stole
The Letter J
by Jabari Mahiri $3.95

The Tiger Who Wore
White Gloves
by Gwendolyn Brooks $5.00

A Sound Investment
by Sonia Sanchez $2.95

I Look At Me
by Mari Evans $2.50

Black Books Bulletin

A limited number of back issues
of this unique journal are available
at $3.00 each:

Vol. 1, Fall '71   Interview with
                    Hoyt W. Fuller

Vol. 1, No. 3   Interview with
                    Lerone Bennett, Jr.

Vol. 5, No. 3   Science & Struggle

Vol. 5, No. 4   Blacks & Jews

Vol. 7, No. 3   The South

Order from **Third World Press**
7524 S. Cottage Grove Ave.
Chicago, IL 60619

Shipping: Add $2.00 for first book
and .25 for each additional book.
Mastercard /Visa orders may be placed
by calling 1-312/651-0700